a gift for

_____

QUEEN

of your own life

IF NOT NOW...WHEN?

Published by Sellers Publishing, Inc.

161 John Roberts Road, South Portland, ME 04106
Visit us at www.sellerspublishing.com • E-mail: rsp@rsvp.com

© 2015 Sellers Publishing, Inc.
Art, design, and text © 2015 Two Belles LLC

ISBN-13: 978-1-4162-4566-7

Printed and bound in China.

10 9 8 7 6 5 4 3 2 1

QUEEN
of your own life
IF NOT NOW...WHEN?

BY KATHY KINNEY & CINDY RATZLAFF

SELLERS
PUBLISHING

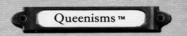

Queenisms ™

She had no doubt it was
going to be a very good year.
Her power and knowledge
were growing steadily every day.

In the Battle for Herself she
had all of the tools necessary
to be victorious.

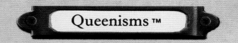
Queenisms ™

She could be gentle,
kind, and loving, but
let no one be fooled!

She was a Warrior Queen
who had the strength
and courage to conquer
all that life tossed her way.

7

Queenisms ™

Her life was a circus.

So she decided to
enjoy the ride.

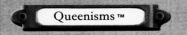
Queenisms ™

When she looked for
goodness, she found
it everywhere.

And so she vowed to
look more often.

Queenisms ™

She didn't really believe
in the word "can't."

So she replaced it
with the phrase
"I just haven't figured
out *how* yet."

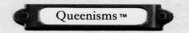
Queenisms ™

Her philosophy was simple.
A judgmental heart was
contrary to a joyful life.
She preferred to illuminate
the good she saw in others.
And, everyone who crossed
her path felt a bit shinier
as a result.

Queenisms ™

She decided to be
herself and let
others do the same.

Life was so much
easier when you
didn't judge.

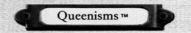

She had a secret
that made her seem
mysterious and exotic
to others. This made
her smile, because her
secret was simply that
she dared to believe:
Her gifts of curiosity
and creativity were
worthy of pursuit.

Queenisms ™

She saw the good
in every person she met.
And her vision was so strong,
they came to see themselves
through her eyes.

Queenisms ™

She couldn't stop second-guessing her every decision.

But when she finally found the courage to take a leap of faith and trust in herself, she was pleased as punch to discover she was pretty darned wise and wonderful.

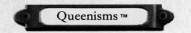

She gave no mind to
the things other people
expected of her, for she
was her own taskmaster
with a breathtakingly
beautiful list of things
she expected of herself.

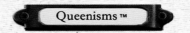
Queenisms ™

She decided to come
from a place of love when
dealing with herself and
everyone else.

Being a loving woman
didn't make her weak;
it made her strong,
resilient, and wise.

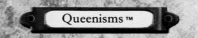
Queenisms ™

She remembered the
adventurous, hopeful,
wildly optimistic girl
she had once been and
invited that girl back
into her life. She was
ready to reclaim her
true self.

Queenisms ™

She tried so hard to
please other people
and make them like
her, that she forgot
that the only one she
really had to please
and love was herself.

She decided she was
done with that rodeo.

31

Queenisms ™

She shook the dust of regret
off her shoes so as not
to track that mess into
her next new adventure.

33

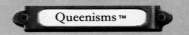

Queenisms ™

It was time for her to
step up and take care of herself.

She decided she needed to open
up a big can of whoop-ass.

Come to think of it, one can
wasn't going to be enough.

Queenisms ™

She wrote herself a
note and tucked it into
her pocket to pull out
whenever she needed it most.

It read:

Dear Me,
That thing you've been
dreaming about doing . . . do it.
You are worth the risk.
Love, Me

Queenisms ™

She realized she'd been
her own harshest critic,
and luckily, she could
stop any old time
she pleased.

So she did.
The ensuing quiet
was delicious.

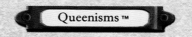
Queenisms ™

She was a disruptive
force of nature, boldly
performing random acts
of altruism, smiling
at strangers, and showing
empathy to everyone she met.

She was a rebel.

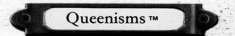

She didn't
always know
where she was going,
but she liked
how she felt
in the driver's seat.

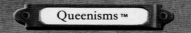

She was a woman
of her word. She
said yes when she
meant yes and no
when she meant no.
Life was too short
for fiddle-faddle.

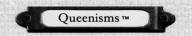
Queenisms ™

She needed to stop thinking
of her life with fear and
instead see it for what it is:

A bold adventure being led
by a very brave woman.

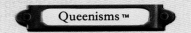
Queenisms ™

The grass was not
greener on the other side.
She knew because
she'd looked.

Turned out happiness was
a practice, not a place.
So she made the choice
to practice every day.

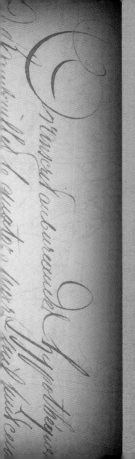

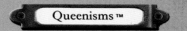
She gave herself the
gift of a daydream.

It was cheaper
than a vacation and
had zero calories.

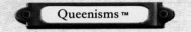
Queenisms™

She understood the
healing power of a
good belly laugh
and incorporated
one into her life
whenever possible.

54

She held this strong
personal philosophy:
There will always be
closets to clean and
work to do, but the moments
of pure fun are fleeting.

So she guarded
those opportunities fiercely
and cherished them
with all her heart.

Queenisms ™

You are hereby awarded
this medal of honor for
getting out of bed
every day and showing
up for life with
courage, humor, and hope.

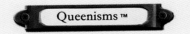
Queenisms ™

It was true; life
could be rough, but
it wasn't anything
she couldn't handle.

All she had to do
was keep her hat on
tight and sit tall in her
saddle; she'd be just fine.

Queenisms ™

She handed in her
resignation. She was
no longer available to
be the acting president of
the People Pleasing Club.

The only approval she
needed was her own.

Queenisms ™

She was the radiant
Queen of her own life.

Her energy was powerful
enough to light up
the whole world.